MARTIAL ARTS

BLAINE WISEMAN

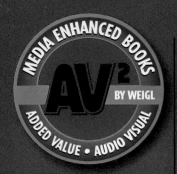

BOOK CODE

N208336

AV² by Weigl brings you media enhanced books that support active learning.

AV² provides enriched content that supplements and complements this book. Weigl's AV² books strive to create inspired learning and engage young minds for a total learning experience.

Go to **www.av2books.com**, and enter this book's unique code. You will have access to video, audio, web links, quizzes, a slide show, and activities.

Audio
Listen to sections of the book read aloud.

Video
Watch informative video clips.

Web Link
Find research sites and play interactive games.

Try This!
Complete activities and hands-on experiments.

Due to the dynamic nature of the Internet, some of the URLs and activities provided as part of AV² by Weigl may have changed or ceased to exist. AV² by Weigl accepts no responsibility for any such changes. All media enhanced books are regularly monitored to update addresses and sites in a timely manner. Contact AV² by Weigl at 1-866-649-3445 or av2books@weigl.com with any questions, comments, or feedback.

Published by AV² by Weigl
350 5th Avenue, 59th Floor
New York, NY 10118
Website: www.av2books.com   www.weigl.com

Library of Congress Cataloging-in-Publication Data

Wiseman, Blaine.
 Martial arts : in the zone / Blaine Wiseman.
    p. cm.
 Includes index.
 ISBN 978-1-60596-910-7 (hard cover : alk. paper) -- ISBN 978-1-60596-911-4 (soft cover : alk. paper) --
 ISBN 978-1-60596-912-1 (e-book)
 1. Martial arts--Juvenile literature. I. Title.
 GV1101.35.W57 2011
 796.8--dc22
                          2009050299

Printed in the United States of America in North Mankato, Minnesota
1 2 3 4 5 6 7 8 9 0   14 13 12 11 10

052010
WEP264000

PROJECT COORDINATOR Heather C. Hudak   DESIGN Terry Paulhus

Every reasonable effort has been made to trace ownership and to obtain permission to reprint copyright material. The publishers would be pleased to have any errors or omissions brought to their attention so that they may be corrected in subsequent printings.

Weigl acknowledges Getty Images as its primary image supplier for this title.

CONTENTS

In the past, martial arts were used in war. Warriors used martial arts to defend themselves against enemies. Today, martial arts have become popular competitive sports and exercise activities.

The most important lesson that all martial arts students learn is self-control.

Martial arts are forms of **self-defense** that were developed over thousands of years in Asia. Most types of martial arts teach people to protect themselves using their hands, arms, feet, legs, and body. All martial arts teach participants to use their skills only for self-defense, not aggression. Participants use their fists and feet for peace rather than violence.

It is unknown where the first martial arts were developed. The ancient Greeks practiced a type of martial art called Pankration. It was a form of wrestling that exercised the entire body. Ancient Egyptians also practiced a form of martial art more than 4,000 years ago. However, the roots of modern martial arts come from the ancient Asian religion of **Buddhism**.

The first Asian martial arts were developed in India, China, and Japan. They grew from breathing exercises that are designed to calm the soul, lower **blood pressure**, and exercise all parts of the body, inside and out. Some martial arts mimic the movements of animals, while others use slow, deliberate movements to help focus the mind and build up "Chi," or life force, adding power to the movements.

Martial arts are much more than the art of fighting. It takes years of study and practice to fully understand any martial art. Learning to punch and kick an opponent is only a small part of martial arts.

Participants must learn **discipline**, patience, and respect. Only after learning these skills, as well as the physical skills involved, will a student progress to the next level.

Martial artists wear headgear to protect their head from injury during **sparring** and in competitions. The headgear is made of thick foam, protecting fighters from serious injury when they are struck in the head.

In most martial arts competitions, the opponents score points by striking each other. The objective is not to injure the opponent. For this reason, martial artists often wear padding on their knees, shoulders, and torso. The padding keeps the opponents safe and makes them focus on technique, rather than striking power.

Some martial arts, such as karate, use colored belts to show the level a student has reached. In karate, white is the lowest level, while black is the highest. The belts can include stripes to show even more levels. There are different degrees of black belts that experts can achieve through additional study and practice.

The main pieces of equipment used in martial arts are the body and mind. Physical and mental strength are the keys to being a skilled martial artist. Different types of martial arts use different pieces of equipment to protect the participants and to define levels of skill.

In most cases, martial artists wear loose-fitting, lightweight clothing. This allows them to move freely while keeping the body cool. **Sparring** equipment is important to protect martial artists while they are training.

Being punched, kicked, thrown, and flipped can be very dangerous, and participants must combine the use of protective equipment and self-defense techniques in order to protect themselves.

■ Some martial arts include weapons training for advanced students. Kendo is the art of Japanese samurai **swordsmanship**. At lower levels of kendo, participants use bamboo practice swords instead of real swords. As the students progress through their training, they are able to use swords made of steel instead of bamboo.

■ Capoeira is a combination of fighting and dancing.

Martial arts are practiced all around the world. Over the centuries, as the arts have spread from country to country and culture to culture, they have taken on many forms of **combat** and self-defense. For example, Indian martial arts often include ideals of India's major religion, Hinduism. Many of the techniques and poses used in Indian martial arts come from yoga. Jiujitsu is a Brazilian martial art that uses skills and theories from Asian martial arts. These are some common types of martials arts.

■ Developed in Korea, *taekwondo* means "the way of the foot and the fist." It involves powerful kicks, punches, spins, and blocks. Students of taekwondo will become faster, stronger, and more flexible and agile.

■ Karate was developed when Chinese martial artists brought their arts to the Japanese island of Okinawa. This form of self-defense relies on strength, fitness, flexibility, **agility**, and mental awareness. Karate, which means "empty hand," teaches students how to react quickly to threats from opponents. Most of the offensive moves in karate involve punching and kicking.

■ Hapkido is the Korean art of self-defense. Concentrating on **pressure points**, it teaches students to use an opponent's strength against them. Hapkido is a way of finding harmony between the body and mind. Students use the art to defend against attacks without using much force or energy.

■ Kung fu is a type of Chinese martial arts that was developed more than 3,000 years ago. The many styles of kung fu are often named after animals, which are used for inspiration. For example, monkey kung fu is based on the movements and fighting techniques of monkeys. It is a fast, hard-hitting martial art that relies on tumbling, lunging, and being sneaky.

■ Tai chi chuan, or tai chi as it is more often called, combines slow movement, meditation, and deep breathing. Tai chi promotes healthy living for both body and mind. This martial art helps people cope with painful diseases, such as **arthritis**, and can help maintain good blood pressure. It can also help with **stress** relief and weight loss.

■ Judo teaches students to defend themselves by flipping, pinning, choking, punching, and kicking their opponent. Students who practice judo will improve their strength as well as their **stamina**.

All martial arts teach patience, respect, and self-defense. Discipline and dedication are the ultimate rules of any martial art. A student can only become a master of martial arts after years of dedicated study and strong discipline. It is important for martial artists to learn that their skills should only be used for self-defense. They are never meant to be used to start a fight.

In martial arts competitions, participants punch, kick, flip, and pin each other. However, there are rules they must follow. In many competitions, participants must bow to the referee and their opponent. This shows that they respect the judge's authority and their opponent's skill. The referee is always in charge of a fight in competitions.

■ In taekwondo, referees control the match. They can penalize a fighter for breaking the rules.

In certain competitions, such as the taekwondo event in the Olympics, fighters wear special padded suits and headgear. The suits are marked with colored circles on target areas. Competitors are awarded points for striking these areas.

In judo, competitors are given points for pinning their opponent on the mat. Another type of martial arts competition features competitors using their hands, feet, elbows, and head to break pieces of wood, bricks, or blocks of ice. These competitions are called "breaking." Competitors must make sure that the items they are attempting to break are solid, without any cracks or breaks.

■ To break boards, an athlete must hit them with as much force as possible and focus the strike on a small area.

In all martial arts competitions, certain parts of the body are illegal to strike on an opponent. Depending on the competition and skill level of the competitors, these can include the groin, the throat, the head, the spine, and the kidneys.

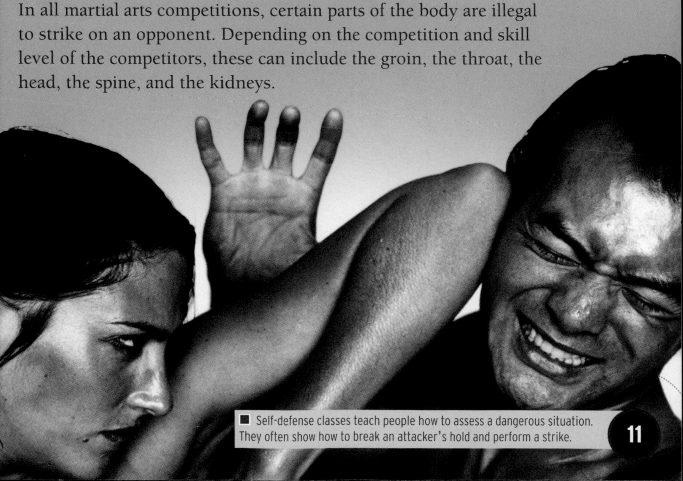

■ Self-defense classes teach people how to assess a dangerous situation. They often show how to break an attacker's hold and perform a strike.

There are many moves that can be learned in each type of martial art. These include kicks, punches, holds, chokes, pins, spins, flips, trips, dodges, and blocks.

Each type of martial art has its own style. While karate, taekwondo, and tai chi all feature kicks, they teach very different styles of kicks. Some types of kicks in karate rely on quickness. This may include snapping the foot at the end of the kick to add whip to the kick.

In taekwondo, a back kick features competitors spinning their body so that their back is facing the target. As they spin, martial artists extend one leg behind them to strike the target. This kick has more force, but it leaves the competitor's back open to attack.

■ The best-known moves in martial arts are punches and kicks. While these are offensive moves, martial artists try to stand in a defensive position while performing them.

■ Choosing the wrong time to perform a move, or performing it improperly, can leave a competitor open to a return blow from his or her opponent.

Tai chi kicks are performed very slowly. The goal is to perform a kick while breathing deeply and slowly. This helps the body and mind work together, improving the participant's focus.

It is important for martial arts students to learn to protect themselves. In addition to using their strength to defeat an opponent, students should also know how to be attacked without being injured.

Many martial arts, such as judo, teach students how to fall so that they are not hurt. As well, students may learn techniques for blocking or dodging an attack. By reacting to an opponent's attack, martial artists can conserve their own energy while their opponent wastes energy striking out.

■ Ukemi, or falling safely, must be mastered first in judo. This helps students avoid injury.

n mixed martial arts (MMA), competitors trained in different types of martial arts fight against each other. Modern mixed martial arts began when traditional martial arts spread around the world.

While pankration is considered a mixed martial art, Brazilian jiujitsu is thought to be the first modern type of mixed martial arts. Many of the moves come from traditional Japanese arts. However, Brazilian jiujitsu is not bound by the traditions of older forms of martial arts.

In 1925, Carlos and Helio Gracie, two brothers from Brazil, opened a martial arts training center in Rio de Janeiro. When Carlos realized the center was running out of money, he put ads in newspapers that said, "If you want a broken arm or rib, contact Carlos Gracie." The challenge changed the world of martial arts.

■ Training for MMA competitions requires a great deal of dedication. Most fighters have to master several fighting styles to succeed.

The Gracie brothers began taking on challengers who specialized in boxing, wrestling, capoeira, and many other fighting styles. The fights became so popular that they had to be held in huge soccer stadiums. Eventually, martial arts masters from Asia began to challenge the Gracies. Helio Gracie, who weighed 135 pounds (61.2 kilograms), became a Brazilian hero. He defeated competitors from around the world who sometimes outweighed him by more than 100 pounds (45.4 kg).

In 1993, Helio Gracie's oldest son, Rorion, started the Ultimate Fighting Championship (UFC). Many UFC competitors are trained in several martial arts styles, which they blend in order to react to different types of attacks. Today, mixed martial arts is one of the most popular professional sports in the United States.

■ Unlike Olympic taekwondo competitions, most modern MMA competitions do not use headgear or pads outside of training.

Martial Arts has some well-known legends.
They have entertained fans and broken records.

Bruce Lee

HOMETOWN: Hong Kong, China
BIRTHDATE: November 27, 1940

CAREER FACTS

- Lee began studying kung fu at the age of 13.
- At the age of 18, Lee took a steamship from Hong Kong to San Francisco with only $100 in his pocket. He quickly moved to Seattle, where he attended university.
- By the time he left Hong Kong, Lee had appeared in 20 movies. He said that his passion was martial arts, but his career choice was acting.
- Lee opened his first kung fu school in Seattle. He then moved to Oakland and Los Angeles, where he opened schools. He taught his style of kung fu, which he called Jeet

Kune Do. This means "The Way of the intercepting fist."
- Lee starred in the Green Hornet, a television series in 1966. He then made more movies in Hong Kong. Lee died on alleged reaction between his out reaction. Enter the Dragon was released in 1973. The movie became Lee's best known and made him an international legend.

Jackie Chan

HOMETOWN: Hong Kong, China
BIRTHDATE: April 7, 1954

CAREER FACTS

- Jackie Chan began practicing kung fu as a young boy. His father would wake him early in the morning and they would practice together, learning discipline, patience, courage, and skill.
- At the age of seven, Chan began attending a school that trained people to perform in Chinese opera. The training included martial arts, singing, dancing, acting, and acrobatics. Chan attended the school for 10 years.

- Chan appeared in his first movie when he was eight years old. As he got older, he appeared in many more movies as an actor and stuntman. He became very popular because he was willing to perform any stunt.
- Chan continues to make movies. He also works for the United Nations, helping people around the world deal with **poverty** and diseases, such as **HIV/AIDS**.

Chuck Norris

HOMETOWN: Ryan, Oklahoma
BIRTHDATE: March 10, 1940

CAREER FACTS

- Norris won the World Professional Karate Championship each year from 1968 until 1974. He retired from the competition **undefeated**.
- He has been named fighter of the year, instructor of the year, and man of the year by the *Black Belt* magazine.
- In 1997, Norris was awarded an eighth degree black belt, making him a grand master of taekwondo. He is the first person from the western hemisphere to achieve the honor.

- Norris has appeared in many movies, including *An Eye for an Eye, Delta Force,* and *Missing in Action*. He also starred on the television series *Walker: Texas Ranger*.
- Norris has set up martial arts classes in schools across the United States.
- He works with war veterans and has helped the United Way raise more than two billion dollars through a television commercial.

Royce Gracie

HOMETOWN: Rio de Janeiro, Brazil and Torrance, California
BIRTHDATE: December 12, 1966

CAREER FACTS

- Gracie comes from the most legendary family in martial arts. His father, Helio, and uncle, Carlos, invented Brazilian jiujitsu. His brother, Rorion, started the UFC.
- Gracie competed in his first tournament when he was eight years old.
- By the time he was 18, Gracie had earned a black belt.
- After Rorion moved to the United States, Royce followed. They taught martial arts classes for hours every day in their garage. Eventually, they opened their own

martial arts school. It became one of the biggest in the country.
- At the first UFC event, "UFC 1," Gracie defeated three opponents in one day to claim the championship. At "UFC 2," he defeated four more fighters to defend his title as the Ultimate Fighter.
- Gracie has instructed thousands of students, including Nicolas Cage, Guy Ritchie, and Chuck Norris.

Many martial artists today are rising stars of the sport.

Jet Li

HOMETOWN: Beijing, China
BIRTHDATE: April 26, 1963

CAREER FACTS

- Li began studying martial arts when he was eight years old. Three years later, he won the Chinese national championship. He would defend his title for five years.
- During this time, Li toured the world, performing martial arts for the Chinese government. He even performed for President Richard Nixon at the White House.
- After retiring from competitive martial arts at 17 years of age, Li began making movies. He has starred in several movies, including *Leathal Weapon 4*, *The One*, and *Romeo Must Die*.
- Li works with charities, such as the Red Cross. His own charity, the One Foundation, helps children in China gain self-respect and discipline.

Gina Carano

Chuck Liddell

HOMETOWN:

BIRTHDATE:

CAREER FACTS

Anderson Silva

HOMETOWN: Curitiba, Brazil
BIRTHDATE: April 14, 1975

CAREER FACTS

- Silva began training in taekwondo at the age of 14. Before this, his family could not afford lessons.
- Silva watched other kids practice jiujitsu and tried to copy their moves.
- He is trained in Muay Thai kickboxing and Brazilian jiujitsu.
- In his first UFC fight, Silva knocked out his opponent in only 49 seconds. In his second fight, he won in under three minutes.

- Silva's nickname is "The Spider." This is because he has long arms and legs and is known for moving with great speed. Silva moves so quickly that his opponents have said he seems to have eight arms and legs.

Martial arts training and competition can be demanding on the body. Martial artists need to work hard to stay strong and healthy. Eating a balanced diet is an important part of staying healthy. A diet with plenty of fruits and vegetables, breads and cereals, and milk and milk products helps keep athletes strong.

It is also important for martial artists to eat enough calories each day. Athletes use up more energy than people who do not exercise as much. Drinking plenty of water before and after exercising is also very important. Athletes need to replace the water they lose through sweating.

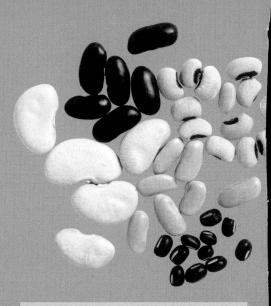

■ Beans are an excellent source of protein, carbohydrates, and vitamins.

■ Without a proper diet, many martial artists may feel weak, both mentally and physically.

Whether they are skilled at their sport or beginners, martial artists need to warm up properly before training or competing. Stretching before and after physical exercise helps prevent muscle strains and injuries.

Martial arts exercise all parts of the body, so it is important to do a thorough stretch before taking part in the sport. Athletes should stretch their arms, legs, back, neck, shoulders, and all other body parts that are being used. After stretching, martial artists will often meditate or concentrate on their breathing to prepare their mind and body for activity.

■ While stretching, it is important that martial artists breathe in slowly through their noses. They hold the breath for a moment, and then, exhale. This helps relax the body.

Test your knowledge of martial arts by trying to answer these brain teasers.

1 What is the name of the ancient Greek martial art?

2 What is the most important lesson that martial arts teach?

3 Name the Brazilian martial art that includes dancing.

4 Who started the UFC?

5 What is the martial art tai chi used for?

6 What is the name of the martial art invented by Bruce Lee?

ANSWERS: 1. Pankration 2. Discipline 3. Capoeira 4. Rorion Gracie 5. Healthy living for both body and mind 6. Jeet Kune Do

Glossary

agility: able to move quickly with good balance

allergic reaction: when the body is damaged by a reaction to a chemical

arthritis: a disease that causes pain in the joints

blood pressure: the force and speed of blood moving through the body

Buddhism: an Asian religion that is based on the teaching of Siddhartha Gautama

combat: fighting

discipline: self-control and a serious attitude

HIV/AIDS: a disease that makes it difficult for the body to fight off sickness

poverty: lack of money or possessions

pressure points: points on the body that are sensitive when pinched or pushed

self-defense: techniques that help people defend themselves against an attack

sparring: a practice match with another martial artist

stamina: the ability to be active for a long period

stress: mental or emotional strain

swordsmanship: being highly skilled and trained using a sword

undefeated: never lost a match

Index

Log on to www.av2books.com

AV² by Weigl brings you media enhanced books that support active learning. Go to **www.av2books.com**, and enter the special code inside the front cover of this book. You will gain access to enriched and enhanced content that supplements and complements this book. Content includes video, audio, web links, quizzes, a slide show, and activities.

Audio
Listen to sections of the book read aloud.

Video
Watch informative video clips.

Web Link
Find research sites and play interactive games.

Try This!
Complete activities and hands-on experiments.

WHAT'S ONLINE?

Try This!
Complete activities and hands-on experiments.

Pages 6-7 Test your knowledge of martial arts equipment.

Pages 8-9 Try to identify the different types of martial arts.

Pages 12-13 See how well you know martial arts moves.

Pages 16-17 Write a biography about one of the superstars of martial arts.

Pages 20-21 Play an interactive game.

Page 22 Test your martial arts knowledge.

Web Link
Find research sites and play interactive games.

Pages 4-5 Find out more information about the history of martial arts.

Pages 8-9 Learn more about the different types of martials arts.

Pages 10-11 Learn more about martial arts competitions.

Pages 12-13 Read about martial arts moves.

Pages 14-15 Learn about the history of mixed martial arts.

Pages 20-21 Find out more about eating well.

Video
Watch informative video clips.

Pages 4-5 Take a video tour through martial arts history.

Pages 18-19 View an interview with one of the world's top martial artists.

EXTRA FEATURES

Audio
Hear introductory audio at the top of every page

Key Words
Study vocabulary, and play a matching word game.

Slide Show
View images and captions, and try a writing activity.

AV² Quiz
Take this quiz to test your knowledge

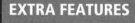